AFRICAN-AMERICAN MUSIC TRIVIA, BOOK I

AFRICAN-AMERICAN MUSIC TRIVIA, BOOK I

Alicia Woodfork-Wilkerson

Word in Due Season Publishing, LLC

AFRICAN-AMERICAN MUSIC TRIVIA BOOK I

Alicia Woodfork-Wilkerson

Copyright ©1997 by Alicia C. Woodfork-Wilkerson
All rights reserved

Word in Due Season Publishing, LLC
P.O. Box 210921
Auburn Hills, Michigan 48321-0921

Cover Design by ET Graphix

ISBN 13: 978-0-9829686-3-5
ISBN 10: 0-9829686-3-5

Library of Congress Control Number: 2014948157

Printed in the United States of America

No part of this book covered by copyrights hereon may be reproduced, stored in or introduced into a retrieval system, or transmitted, in any form, or by any means (electronic, mechanical, photocopying, recording or otherwise), without the prior written permission of the copyright owner.

I dedicate this book to five very special and important role models who is and was a part of my life. Without them, I would not be who I am today. I thank God for blessing me with their unconditional love, support, influence and the drive to pursue all of my dreams:

My mother, Willie Mae McCoy-Johnson
My husband, Martin Wilkerson (deceased)
My father, Robert Johnson (deceased)
My maternal grandmother, Elizabeth Rushton-Scott (deceased)
My maternal grandfather, Joseph Scott (deceased)

ACKNOWLEDGMENTS

First, I thank God for the gift of writing. I realize that for many, writing is a difficult and daunting challenge. For me, whether it is a simple letter, a report or a speech, the words have always come easily to me when it is time to write. That is how I know that it is a gift and one of the many talents my Lord and Savior blessed me with. I pray that this labor of love is pleasing in His sight.

Mama, you are my biggest cheerleader and supporter. You were the first heart that loved me and to this very day, you have given your love and support in everything I set out to do. If I could write for the next 100 years non-stop, it wouldn't be enough time for me to write everything you mean to me, how you have influenced my life and how much I love you. Thank you for loving and believing in me. You are my hero!

Sam Anderson, Jr., thank you for your unwavering support, unconditional love and understanding with the many things I have undertaken in my life as well as those things I didn't see coming. I have faced, at times, enormous responsibilities that would shake the average woman. Through it all, you have been there to support me by offering advice, constructive criticism and a shoulder to lean on when I needed it most. I love you.

My brothers Brian and Avery; my sister-in-law Marshall, my niece and nephew, Psalms and Avery II, my great nieces Solai, Skye, my great nephews, Saviion, Spencyr, Sy and my sister from other parents, Alma; plain and simple: I love you all.

Dr. Jerome Branham, thank you for the many talks we had about our books and our desire to write bestselling books and devote our lives to writing full-time during my many visits to your office over the years. Your encouragement, support and friendship mean the world to me.

David Zanin, my dear friend, co-worker, U.S. Army Veteran and owner of Zanin's Creative Photography in Oxford, Michigan; thank you for the awesome photographs! Your passion, understanding and creativity shines brightly through every photo. What was supposed to be a few shots for a headshot turned into a two-hour photo session with the most amazing photographs that I have ever taken. It was a blast and I was blown away with the finished photographs! It was hard for me to decide which one to use for my book. Thank you for the awesome photo. I thank you, Dave, for making me look like a true "Rock Star". I love you, my Buddy.

I want to acknowledge and thank you, the student; the trivia buff; the music lover, for undertaking this journey with me on what is my first published book. I hope that everyone who touches it will enjoy the challenge the same way that it touched me.

Last but not least, by any measure, I have to thank my publisher, editor and dear friend, Darliss Batchelor for all of her hard work, timely editing, direction and support. Darliss, you made a 17 year-old dream finally come true for me. You put your writing projects aside and took time out of your already hectic schedule to make something that was on my Bucket List become a reality. Thank you for all that you have done. I am so very appreciative and thankful that God directed me to you. I've got nothing but love for you.

TABLE OF CONTENTS

Introduction

RHYTHM AND BLUES/SOUL PART I
THE EARLY YEARS
1950-1965

Name the Artist	18
What Were Our Original Names?	21
Name the Year	22
The Name Game and Birthplace	27

RHYTHM AND BLUES/SOUL PART II
THE NEXT 15 YEARS
1966-1981

Number Ones	38
Grab Bag	44

RHYTHM AND BLUES/SOUL PART III
END OF THE CENTURY
1982-1996

In the Know	48
Match Up	52

AMERICAN JAZZ ERA

Jazz Grab Bag	56

AFRICAN-AMERICAN GOSPEL

Who Are We?	64

THE DISCO ERA

Disco Song Titles	70

RAP

"Rap" It Up	74
It's a "Rap"	78
A.K.A. (Also Known As)	80

THE BLUES

Name the Artist   84

A.K.A. (Also Known As)   88

MOVIE SOUNDTRACKS/TELEVISION THEME SONGS

You Name It   92

MULTIPLE MUSIC GENRES

Dearly Departed   100

Answers   107

Source References   128

INTRODUCTION

Do you like music?

Music is a part of everyday life. Whether we are in our cars or in the privacy of our homes, very few of us resist the temptation to turn the knob, flip the switch or press the button on our stereo systems to listen to the old 45's, cassette tapes, CD's and for a few of us, our 8-Track tape players, to enjoy the sounds that make us happy, melancholy, adventurous, romantic or nostalgic.

We listen to and enjoy music for various reasons. Because of society's love of music, we have made music an important and essential part of our lives. Most of us have one or many songs that remind of us of memorable events, that special someone, songs that make us pat our feet or snap our fingers. Music is a part of our culture. Many radio shows and news broadcasts worldwide have included in their programming format trivia questions that members of their listening and viewing audience may answer to win cash prizes, concert and sporting event tickets or just to serve as a medium to challenge their listeners and viewers knowledge of music and the history behind the artists. Many colleges and universities have courses that focus specifically on music's roots and history as well as the vast number of gifted, complex and unique artists that influenced music's rich history.

African-American Music Trivia, Book I will take you on a trivia journey through various music genres (Rhythm & Blues, Jazz, Gospel, Blues, Rap, and even Disco). The selections are multiple choice and question and answer (fill in the blank). There are questions pertaining to movie soundtracks, name the artist, song titles, A.K.A. (Also Known As). There's even a section, "Dearly Departed", which will test the reader's knowledge on where or how some of our favorite artists passed away. The difference in African-American Music Trivia, Book I is that it may be used in Music History courses as a workbook, as a source of entertainment with family, friends, or individually.

It is because of my enjoyment of music and my love of trivia in general that I was inspired to create this book. I believe *African-American Music Trivia, Book I* will bring to those who utilize the book, whether as a learning tool or just a fun book for music trivia buffs, the many hours of entertainment and music education that I received while creating it.

RHYTHM AND BLUES/SOUL PART I
The Early Years 1950-1965

African-American Music Trivia

NAME THE ARTIST *Answers page 108*

1. What artist outsold every artist in the 1950s except Elvis Presley?
   a   Fats Domino
   b   Little Richard
   c   Lou Rawls
   d   Percy Sledge

2. Two of his hits were "Tutti-Frutti" and "Long Tall Sally".
   a   Robert Johnson
   b   Otis Redding
   c   Little Richard
   d   Eddie Floyd

3. What female group hit the charts in 1962 with the song, "He's A Rebel"?
   a   The Emotions
   b   The Crystals
   c   The Chiffons
   d   The Supremes

4. The song, "Sixty Minute Man" was a hit in 1951 for this doo-wop group.
   a   Billy Ward and The Dominoes
   b   The Intruders
   c   The Floaters
   d   The Coasters

Rhythm & Blues/Soul Part I

5. What was the name of the group that recorded the 1961 hit, "Little Egypt"?
   a   The Coasters
   b   The Temptations
   c   The Dells
   d   Ray, Goodman and Brown

6. "Just One Look" was all it took for this artist in 1963. Who was she?
   a   Telma Hopkins
   b   Anita Baker
   c   Barbara Lewis
   d   Doris Troy

7. What group recorded the 1954 hit, "Gloria"?
   a   The Chryslers
   b   The Cadillacs
   c   The Packards
   d   The Plymouths

8. Name the group that recorded the 1955 smash hit, "Only You (And You Alone)".
   a   The Isley Brothers
   b   The Platters
   c   The 5 Royales
   d   The Dramatics

African-American Music Trivia

9. This group scored it big with the 1960 hit, "Save the Last Dance for Me".
   a   The Bar-Kays
   b   The Drifters
   c   Cameo
   d   The O'Jays

10. These ladies released the 1961 hit, "Please Mr. Postman". Name the group.
    a   The Marvelettes
    b   The Daiseys
    c   The Shirelles
    d   The Three Degrees

Rhythm & Blues/Soul Part I

WHAT WERE OUR ORIGINAL NAMES?
Answers page 108

Provide the names of the following groups as they were known **before** they made it big.

11. The Cardinals

12. The Bobbettes

13. The Five Keys

14. The Dixie Cups

15. The Main Ingredient

16. The Chiffons

17. The Miracles

18. The Delphonics

19. The Ikettes

20. The Clovers

NAME THE YEAR *Answers page 109*

21. "Maybelline" by Chuck Berry
    - a   1953
    - b   1955
    - c   1958
    - d   1960

22. "The Bells" by The Dominoes
    - a   1950
    - b   1953
    - c   1954
    - d   1957

23. "The Twist" by Chubby Checker
    - a   1960
    - b   1963
    - c   1964
    - d   1965

24. "Shake A Hand" by Faye Adams
    - a   1951
    - b   1953
    - c   1957
    - d   1959

Rhythm & Blues/Soul Part I

25. "Twist and Shout" by The Isley Brothers
    a   1961
    b   1962
    c   1963
    d   1964

26. "Stand By Me" by Ben E. King
    a   1958
    b   1959
    c   1961
    d   1965

27. "Why Do Fools Fall in Love" by Frankie Lymon and The Teenagers
    a   1951
    b   1952
    c   1956
    d   1957

28. "Look In My Eyes" by The Chantels
    a   1952
    b   1960
    c   1961
    d   1965

29. "Shouldn't I Know" by The Cardinals
    a   1951
    b   1958
    c   1960
    d   1961

30. "You're Gonna Make Me Cry" by O.V. Wright
    a   1958
    b   1960
    c   1963
    d   1965

31. "What Kind of Fool" by The Tams
    a   1954
    b   1959
    c   1963
    d   1965

32. "Do You Love Me?" by The Contours
    a   1960
    b   1961
    c   1962
    d   1965

33. "Baby I Need Your Loving" by The Four Tops
    a   1958
    b   1960
    c   1963
    d   1965

Rhythm & Blues/Soul Part I

34. "Hit the Road, Jack" by Ray Charles
    a   1961
    b   1963
    c   1964
    d   1965

35. "Oh, What A Night" by The Dells
    a   1956
    b   1958
    c   1961
    d   1962

36. "Sexy Ways" by Hank Ballard and The Midnighters
    a   1951
    b   1954
    c   1955
    d   1958

37. "Nowhere to Run" by Martha and The Vandellas
    a   1960
    b   1961
    c   1962
    d   1965

38. "In the Midnight Hour" by Wilson Pickett
    a   1961
    b   1963
    c   1964
    d   1965

39. "Don't Make Me Over" by Dionne Warwick
    a   1961
    b   1962
    c   1963
    d   1964

40. "Oh No, Not My Baby" by Maxine Brown
    a   1958
    b   1960
    c   1964
    d   1965

Rhythm & Blues/Soul Part I

THE NAME GAME AND BIRTHPLACE
Answers page 110

Circle the following artists' birth name and the city in which they were born.

41. **Doris Troy**
    a   Doris Long
    b   Doris Day
    c   Doris Payne
    d   Doris Duke

41a. a   New York City, New York
      b   Detroit, Michigan
      c   Chicago, Illinois
      d   Los Angeles, California

42. **Little Anthony of The Imperials**
    a   Anthony Johnson
    b   Anthony Gourdine
    c   Anthony Grant
    d   Anthony Jackson

42a. a   Queens, New York
      b   Brooklyn, New York
      c   Camden, New Jersey
      d   New York City, New York

African-American Music Trivia

43. **Smokey Robinson**
    a   Robert Robinson
    b   William Robinson
    c   Daniel Robinson
    d   Randall Robinson

43a. a   Philadelphia, Pennsylvania
     b   Detroit, Michigan
     c   Cleveland, Ohio
     d   Southfield, Michigan

44. **Little Eva**
    a   Eva Roberta Jones
    b   Eva Marie Knight
    c   Eva Narcissus Boyd
    d   Eva Lorene Wilson

44a. a   Scott, Mississippi
     b   Bellhaven, North Carolina
     c   Louisville, Kentucky
     d   Montgomery, Alabama

45. **Della Reese**
    a   Della Reese Jackson
    b   Della Mae McCoy
    c   Delloreese Patricia Early
    d   Della Irene Jones

Rhythm & Blues/Soul Part I

45a.   a   Detroit, Michigan
       b   Cleveland, Ohio
       c   Chicago, Illinois
       d   Miami, Florida

46.   **Ray Charles**
       a   Charles Ray
       b   Charles Ray Nelson
       c   Ray Charles Robinson
       d   Ray Charles Randolph

46a.   a   Albany, Georgia
       b   Mexico, Missouri
       c   Baton Rouge, Louisiana
       d   Dallas, Texas

47.   **Ben E. King**
       a   Benjamin Ernest King
       b   Benjamin Earl Nelson
       c   Benjamine Edward King
       d   Benjamin Eliot King

47a.   a   Fort Worth, Texas
       b   Houston, Texas
       c   Natchez, Mississippi
       d   Henderson, North Carolina

African-American Music Trivia

48. Ernie K-Doe
    a   Ernie Doe
    b   Ernie Kay
    c   Ernest Kador, Jr.
    d   Ernest K. Doe, Jr.

48a.
    a   New Baltimore, Michigan
    b   Compton, California
    c   New Orleans, Louisiana
    d   San Diego, California

49. Fats Domino
    a   Antione Domino
    b   John Hall
    c   Jerry Carter
    d   Richard Domino

49a.
    a   New Orleans, Louisiana
    b   San Francisco, California
    c   Flint, Michigan
    d   St. Louis, Missouri

50. Little Richard
    a   Richard James
    b   Richard Jones
    c   Richard Wayne Penniman
    d   Richard Jerome Davis

Rhythm & Blues/Soul Part I

50a.   a   Tallahassee, Florida
       b   Birmingham, Alabama
       c   Nashville, Tennessee
       d   Macon, Georgia

51.   **Stevie Wonder**
       a   Steven Wright
       b   Steven Washington
       c   Steveland Morris
       d   Steven Williams

51a.   a   Kalamazoo, Michigan
       b   Detroit, Michigan
       c   Saginaw, Michigan
       d   Ann Arbor, Michigan

52.   **O.V. Wright**
       a   Ophelius Vernon Wright
       b   Overton Vertis Wright
       c   Otis Verne Worden
       d   Othel Vincent Worden

52a.   a   Charlotte, North Carolina
       b   Leno, Tennessee
       c   Eden, Mississippi
       d   Little Rock, Arkansas

African-American Music Trivia

53. **Chuck Berry**
    a   Charles Berry
    b   Chuckie Edwards
    c   Charles Edward Anderson Berry
    d   Charles Berry Anderson

53a. a   Memphis, Tennessee
       b   San Jose, California
       c   Lubbock, Texas
       d   Pittsburgh, Pennsylvania

54. **Johnny Ace**
    a   John Avant
    b   Johnny Jordan
    c   John Marshall Alexander, Jr.
    d   Johnny Archer

54a. a   Taos, New Mexico
       b   Las Vegas, Nevada
       c   Nassau, Bahamas
       d   Memphis, Tennessee

55. **Brook Benton**
    a   Benton Brooks
    b   Benjamin Franklin Peay
    c   Brook Burton
    d   Barry Benton

Rhythm & Blues/Soul Part I

55a.   a   Hollywood, California
        b   Greenville, North Carolina
        c   Portsmouth, Virginia
        d   Camden, South Carolina

56.   **Bo Diddley**
        a   Ellas Otha Bates McDaniels
        b   Bob Dillon
        c   Robert Woodley
        d   Bo Shannon Woods

56a.   a   Washington, D.C.
        b   Omaha, Nebraska
        c   McComb, Mississippi
        d   Lafayette, Louisiana

57.   **Gene Chandler**
        a   Eugene Chandler
        b   Eugene Dixon
        c   Eugene Harper
        d   Eugene Boyd

57a.   a   Atlanta, Georgia
        b   Chicago, Illinois
        c   San Francisco, California
        d   Green Bay, Wisconsin

African-American Music Trivia

58. **Esther Phillips**
    a   Esther Mae Jones
    b   Ester Coles
    c   Esther Marie Lloyd
    d   Ester Murray

58a. a   Indianapolis, Indiana
       b   Galveston, Texas
       c   Dayton, Ohio
       d   Seattle, Washington

59. **Edwin Starr**
    a   Edward Starr
    b   Corey Edward Devine
    c   Charles Edwin Hatcher
    d   Edwin Avery Keith

59a. a   Hanceville, Alabama
       b   Nashville, Tennessee
       c   Livingston, Alabama
       d   Englewood, New Jersey

60. **Little Willie John**
    a   William Edgar John
    b   William John Edgar
    c   John Williamson
    d   John William Holt

Rhythm & Blues/Soul Part I

60a.   a   Washington, D.C
      b   Louisville, Kentucky
      c   Jacksonville, Florida
      d   Cullendale, Arkansas

RHYTHM AND BLUES/SOUL PART II
The Next 15 Years
1966-1981

African-American Music Trivia

NUMBER ONES *Answers page 112*

Select the year that the following artist(s) released hits on the Rhythm & Blues Chart.

61. "Give It to Me Baby" by Rick James
    a   1978
    b   1979
    c   1980
    d   1981

62. "Feel Like Makin' Love" by Roberta Flack
    a   1970
    b   1971
    c   1973
    d   1974

63. "Tighten Up" by Archie Bell & The Drells
    a   1968
    b   1972
    c   1973
    d   1976

64. "Turn Back the Hands of Time" by Tyrone Davis
    a   1966
    b   1968
    c   1970
    d   1972

65. "You Got the Love" by Rufus featuring Chaka Khan
    a   1967
    b   1969
    c   1974
    d   1975

66. "Back Stabbers" by The O'Jays
    a   1972
    b   1974
    c   1978
    d   1979

67. "One In A Million You" by Larry Graham
    a   1973
    b   1978
    c   1980
    d   1981

68. "Oh Girl" by The Chi-Lites
    a   1967
    b   1968
    c   1970
    d   1972

69. "Lady Marmalade" by LaBelle
    a   1971
    b   1972
    c   1974
    d   1976

70. "Best of My Love" by The Emotions
    a   1975
    b   1977
    c   1979
    d   1981

71. "Sophisticated Lady" by Natalie Cole
    a   1967
    b   1974
    c   1976
    d   1977

72. "Outa-Space" by Billy Preston
    a   1970
    b   1971
    c   1972
    d   1973

73. "September" by Earth, Wind & Fire
    a   1969
    b   1976
    c   1978
    d   1980

74. "Celebration" by Kool & The Gang
    a   1975
    b   1977
    c   1980
    d   1981

75. "You'll Never Find Another Love Like Mine" by Lou Rawls
    a   1968
    b   1970
    c   1974
    d   1976

76. "Cowboy to Girls" by The Intruders
    a   1968
    b   1970
    c   1972
    d   1974

77. "Tryin' to Love Two" by William Bell
    a   1969
    b   1971
    c   1974
    d   1976

78. "We Are Family" by Sister Sledge
    a   1974
    b   1975
    c   1977
    d   1979

79. "The Hustle" by Van McCoy
    a   1969
    b   1971
    c   1973
    d   1975

80. "Burn Rubber (Why You Wanna Hurt Me)" by The Gap Band
    a   1970
    b   1974
    c   1978
    d   1980

81. "In the Rain" by The Dramatics
    a   1972
    b   1973
    c   1975
    d   1978

82. "Don't Stop 'Til You Get Enough" by Michael Jackson
    a   1977
    b   1978
    c   1979
    d   1980

Rhythm & Blues/Soul Part II

83. "Flashlight" by Parliament/Funkadelic
    - a   1975
    - b   1976
    - c   1977
    - d   1978

84. "The Second Time Around" by Shalamar
    - a   1976
    - b   1979
    - c   1980
    - d   1981

85. "L-O-V-E" by Al Green
    - a   1972
    - b   1973
    - c   1975
    - d   1977

African-American Music Trivia

GRAB BAG *Answers page 113*

86. This composer/musician wrote the theme song for the '70s sitcom, *Sanford and Son.*

87. Name the group that songstress Anita Baker sang with before pursuing a solo career.

88. What year did Stevie Wonder release his *Songs in the Key of Life* album?

89. Name the television dance show that MFSB performed the theme song.

90. What does "MFSB" stand for?

91. This male group declared "Heaven Must Be Missing an Angel" in 1976. Name the group.

92. This musical family had a "Hot Line" for love in 1976. Who were they?

93. This group's name was a distress symbol. Name the group.

94. This funk group was a part of a "Family Affair" in 1971. Who were they?

Rhythm & Blues/Soul Part II

95. Name the record label that was co-founded by composer/arranger/recording artists Curtis Mayfield.

96. This album was Stevie Wonder's very first platinum.

97. Jeffrey Daniel, Jody Watley and Gary Mumford were the original members of this group. Name the group.

98. Betty Wright won a Grammy in 1974 for this hit. What was it?

99. This 1971 hit song by Marvin Gaye was about the ecology.

100. He is the lead singer of the Philadelphia group, The Stylistics.

RHYTHM AND BLUES/SOUL PART III
End of the Decade
1981-1996

African-American Music Trivia

IN THE KNOW *Answers page 114*

Supply the correct answer to the following questions.

101. This duo produced Janet Jackson's 1989 *Rhythm Nation 1814* album.

102. This songstress was dubbed the "First Lady" of LaFace Records in Atlanta, Georgia.

103. Frankie Beverly & Maze scored its first number one hit with this song in 1985.

104. This male vocalist was known as the *"Teddy Bear"*.

105. This male trio, who perfected the "New Jack Swing" style, wanted to "Get With U" on their second and final album.

106. This famed guitarist was once married to former Cosby kid Lisa Bonet.

107. Who was the mother of the guitarist named above?

108. Jermaine Jackson was once married to Motown founder Berry Gordy, Jr.'s daughter. What is her name?

Rhythm & Blues/Soul Part III

109. This female vocalist's debut album was *Diamond Life* in 1985.

110. What year did Tina Turner release her comeback hit, "What's Love Got to Do With It"?

111. In 1995, this father/son duo performed a remake of actress Bette Midler's hit, "Wind Beneath My Wings". Name the duo.

112. In 1986, Kool & The Gang declared this was solid as a rock. What was it?

113. El DeBarge and The DeBarge Family are from this mid-western city.

114. This group did a 1986 remake of the Bill Withers 1972 hit, "Lean On Me".

115. What kind of beret did this girl wear in this 1985 song by Prince?

116. What are the first names of the original members of the group, New Edition?

117. This singer/songwriter/producer didn't see "nothing wrong" with a little "Bump & Grind". Who is he?

118. What are the first names of the ladies who formed the 1980s group, Vanity 6?

African-American Music Trivia

119. What album of Patti LaBelle's was the song, "Kiss Away the Pain" featured?

120. Rick James founded this female group, which was named after one of his hit songs.

121. This actor/singer/songwriter wrote the 1971 hit, "Never Can Say Goodbye" for the Jackson 5.

122. What international model that was once married to basketball star Spencer Haywood and is now married to singer David Bowie was featured in Jermaine Jackson's 1984 video for the song, "Do What You Do"?

123. This R&B female group's second album was entitled, "Funky Divas". Name the group.

124. This singer/model/actress, who was born in Kingston, Jamaica, was a "Slave to the Rhythm".

125. She teamed up with Keith Sweat on the song, "Make It Last Forever".

126. This singer/actress and former teenage star was a regular on the ABC sitcom, *Thea* and starred in her own UPN Television sitcom.

Rhythm & Blues/Soul Part III

127. This female vocalist, who is married to actor Flex Alexander (Mark Alexander Knox), released the song, "I Love Your Smile" in 1991. What is her first name?

128. What is the above named vocalist's maiden name?

129. In 1992, this male trio did a remake of the love ballad, "Baby, I'm For Real", written by Marvin Gaye and Ann-Gordy Gaye, which was originally recorded by the Originals in 1967. Name the trio.

130. This 1977 song was the first big hit for the group, Slave. Name the song.

African-American Music Trivia

MATCH UP *Answers page 115*

List the number that matches with the correct artist.

____Undisputed Truth

____Chairmen of the Board

____Heatwave

____Rose Royce

____The Ohio Players

____L.T.D.

____Johnnie Taylor

____Rick James

____Ike & Tina Turner

____Harold Melvin and the Blue Notes

____Special Delivery

____Brothers Johnson

____Phyllis Hyman

____Peaches & Herb

____Candi Staton

Rhythm & Blues/Soul Part III

1. "Young Hearts Run Free"
2. "Car Wash"
3. "Smiling Faces"
4. "Boogie Nights"
5. "Funky Worm"
6. "Somewhere In My Lifetime"
7. "Strawberry Letter 23"
8. "Reunited"
9. "Give Me Just A Little More Time"
10. "The Love I Lost"
11. "River Deep - Mountain High"
12. "Give It To Me Baby"
13. "Somebody's Been Sleeping In My Bed"
14. "Love Ballad"
15. "The Lonely One"

AMERICAN JAZZ ERA

JAZZ GRAB BAG *Answers page 116*

131. Who discovered jazz legend Milt Jackson?

132. Name one of two jazz LP's released by Bill Cosby.

133. This artist recorded "She's Making Whoopee in Hell Tonight".

134. Along with his brothers Melvin and Kellis, this artist played in his uncle's band Bobby Butler and The Mighty Blue Notes.

135. This female jazz singer was five years old when she made her debut at the Apollo Theater in Harlem. Name the artist.

136. Name the artist whose 1967 LP was entitled, *Mama Too Tight*.

137. What year did jazz vocalist Sarah Vaughn join Billy Eckstine's band?

138. On June 19, 1925, Josephine Baker debuted as the star of *Folies Bergére*. Name the club where the performance was held.

American Jazz Era

139. Name the artist that released the 1962 hit, "I've Got a Woman".

140. Two of this jazz man's LPs were *Out to Lunch* and *Music Matador*.

141. What was the first style of music jazz great Herbie Hancock studied?

142. This jazz trumpeter soloed on an early Duke Ellington piece entitled, "Rockin' in Rhythm".

143. What three wood wind instruments is jazz man James Moody considered a master of?

144. Name the year jazz pianist Ramsey Lewis formed the Ramsey Lewis Trio, along with bassist Eldee Young and Red Holt.

145. This jazz pianist is best known for his work with jazz trumpeter Wynton Marsalis and rock star Sting.

146. This jazz saxophonist originally wanted to be a painter, but eventually became a jazz great. He is known for the 1956 LP, "Saxophone Colossus" Who is he?

147. Name the jazz band that Thaddeus "Thad" Jones formed in Denmark in 1978.

African-American Music Trivia

148. This jazz guitarist studied music at Princeton University and graduated in 1981.

149. What year did Billie Holiday begin recording with the Teddy Wilson Orchestra?

150. Name the clarinetist/jazz soloist who formed the New Orleans Feetwarmers Band in 1932.

151. What is jazz pianist Ahmad Jamal's birth name?

152. This jazz trumpeter wrote the score for actor/director Spike Lee's 1991 movie, *Jungle Fever* and his 1992 movie, *Malcolm X*.

153. This jazz bassist married "First Lady of Jazz", Ella Fitzgerald in 1949. Who was he?

154. With what jazz artist did saxophonist Joe Henderson co-lead the Jazz Communicators?

155. This female jazz great died in 1937 and did not receive a headstone until the late rock star Janis Joplin purchased one.

156. What year was pianist/composer Cecil Taylor born?

157. What two string instruments did Stanley Clark study as a child?

American Jazz Era

158. John Coltrane, Philly Joe Jones, Red Garland and Paul Chambers rounded out this jazz legend's first quintet. Name the legend that completed the group.

159. What year did keyboardist/author/poet Gil Scott-Heron release "Legend in His Own Mind"?

160. This female jazz vocalist/keyboardist released the 1982 hit single, "Forget Me Nots".

161. Name the two artists that completed the first Oscar Peterson Trio.

162. What instrument is Freddie Hubbard best known for?

163. This jazz drummer is the brother of jazz artists Thad and Hank Jones.

164. Who was the composer of the jazz standard, "Misty"?

165. How old was jazz singer Carmen McRae when she wrote the song, "Dream of Life".

166. Name the artist who performed the bass licks for Bobby Darin's classic hit, "Mack the Knife".

167. This trumpeter/vocalist/percussionist was a co-founder of the Art Ensemble of Chicago along with jazz artist Roscoe Mitchell.

African-American Music Trivia

168. Name the artist who replaced Joe Zawinul in Maynard Ferguson's Orchestra in 1959.

169. Name the year jazz saxophonist Ornette Coleman and trumpeter Don Cherry released their first LP, *Something Else*.

170. Two of this jazz bassist's LPs are *Bohemia After Dark* and *Blue Brothers*.

171. Where was jazz bassist Charles Mingus born?

172. How many times has composer/producer/arranger Quincy Jones, Jr. been nominated for a Grammy Award as of 1991?

173. This coronet player was said to be the very first jazz musician. Who was he?

174. Name the first tune that "First Lady of Jazz" Ella Fitzgerald recorded.

175. Name the big band that jazz drummer Art Blakey formed in 1947.

176. Name the jazz bassist who holds a Master's degree in music and is a graduate of the Eastman School of Music.

American Jazz Era

177. What year did Duke Ellington and his Orchestra perform at Carnegie Hall for the very first time?

178. What year did Count Basie originally record the song, "One O'Clock Jump"?

179. Name the band that Louis Armstrong formed in 1935.

180. What quartet is jazz bassist Percy Heath a founding member?

AFRICAN-AMERICAN GOSPEL

African-American Music Trivia

WHO ARE WE? *Answers page 118*

181. This female vocalist, who also sings R&B, sang with the 1970s R&B group The Honey Cones and released the 1989 album, *The Search Is Over.*

182. This native Detroiter sang the theme song for the television series, *Amen,* which starred the late Sherman Hemsley and Clifton Davis.

183. This popular Mississippi quartet originally consisted of Archie Brownlee, Joseph Ford, Lawrence Abrams and Lloyd Woodard, and then became a quintet when Melvin Henderson joined.

184. This gospel duo, who released the album, *Rough Side of the Mountain* in 1983, were also pastors. Name the duo.

185. Name the four members who make up the gospel group, The Truthettes.

186. This male gospel singer was once called the "Thunderbolt of the Midwest".

187. These three sisters began singing at the Morning Star Baptist Church in Chicago when they were children during the 1940s. One of their albums is *What Will You Do With Your Life.* Who are they?

African-American Gospel

188. This acapella co-ed group from Alabama was formed during the 1930s and was known for the 1937 hit, "Tone the Bell".

189. This artist is probably better known for his falsetto voice as co-lead for the urban R&B group, Earth, Wind and Fire than a gospel singer. Who is he?

190. She was known as the "Gospel Queen".

191. This Black gospel vocalist formed the group, The Caravans, in 1951, but went on later to a promising solo career. Who is it?

192. This gospel group was formed by James Davis in the late 1920s and sang backup on Paul Simon's 1973 hit, "Love Me Like A Rock". Name the group.

193. This spiritual singer's nickname is "Songbird". Who is she?

194. These brothers were pupils of Mary Johnson Davis and sang with The Greater Harvest Choir during the 1960s. Who are they?

195. What are Grammy Award winners BeBe and CeCe Winans first names?

African-American Music Trivia

196. This gospel vocalist was a former back-up singer for Aretha Franklin, Chaka Khan and B.B. King. She also toured with the play, *Hair*. Who is she?

197. This group was known as a "walking rhythm" quartet. Who are they?

198. This female vocalist formally sang commercial jingles and is the younger sister of Vanessa Bell Armstrong. Who is she?

199. This gospel group was led by tenor Billy Williams, who later sang lead for the Billy Williams Quartet.

200. This gospel performer is a seasoned drummer and the twin sister of another gospel great, Andrae Crouch. Who is she?

201. This gospel artist, known as "The Professor", sang with The Birdettes, The Harmoneers and was known for the hit, "Walking With The King".

202. This artist once led the Jackson Southernaires and maintained his own group, The Messengers. Who is he?

203. Name the gospel group that was the first traditional singers to add rock, jazz and soul to their music.

204. This Detroit-based sister group, who released the 1987 hit, "You Brought The Sunshine", consists of Dorinda, Karen, Twinkie and Jackie. Who are they?

THE DISCO ERA

African-American Music Trivia

DISCO SONG TITLES *Answers page 119*

Complete the names of the following Disco song titles.

205. Last _____

206. Heaven Must Be _____

207. I Will _____

208. Burnin' _____

209. Love _____

210. Good _____

211. He's The _____

212. Don't Stop 'Til _____

213. Boogie _____

214. Open _____

215. Disco _____

216. Everybody _____

The Disco Era

217. Rigor _____

218. Let The Music _____

219. Le _____

220. Love To Love _____

221. Ring My _____

222. Give Me _____

223. YM _____

224. You Make Me Feel _____

225. Got To Be _____

226. Boogie Oogie _____

227. Lady _____

228. Shake Your Groove _____

229. Get _____

230. Hot _____

231. Don't Leave Me _____

African-American Music Trivia

232. Ladies' _____

233. Star _____

234. Rock With _____

RAP

"RAP" IT UP *Answers page 120*

235. This 1979 hit was the first rap song that received widespread attention and helped launch the rap genre. Name the song and the artist.

236. This big hit was featured on Positive K's 1992 album, "*Da Skills Dat Pay Da* Bills". Name the song.

237. What was Gang Starr's debut album?

238. This group released the 1985 hit, "The Show (Oh My God)".

239. This group hailed from Brownsville, Tennessee and was led by Speech.

240. What does L.L. Cool J (moniker for rapper James Smith) stand for?

241. This rap artist appeared in the Mario Van Peebles Black cowboy film *Posse* and in pop/rock superstar Madonna's photo book, *Sex*. Name the artist.

242. This rap duo was known for wearing their clothes backwards when they first came on the music scene. Who were they?

Rap

243. This Brooklyn-based group was accused of performing unsolicited campaign work for David Dinkins' 1993 mayoral campaign. Name the group.

244. What is M.C. Hammer's real name?

245. What was the name of Ice Cube's posse?

246. This rap artist was sued when he allegedly used a sample of "Alone Again, Naturally" by Gilbert O'Sullivan in one of his songs. Who is he?

247. This hot single by Sir Mix-A-Lot was released in the summer of 1992 from his 1991 album, *Mack Daddy*, paying homage to women with large buttocks and putting down women with small ones. Name the single.

248. This artist is considered one of rap's first crossover stars. One of his biggest hits was "The Breaks". Name the artist.

249. Give the stage names of the Furious Five who rapped along with Grandmaster Flash.

250. This rapper once backed Tone-Loc before striking out on his own. His debut album was *Ain't No Shame In My Game*. Name the artist.

African-American Music Trivia

251. Dr. Dre, Michele and Arabian Prince once belonged to this group.

252. The late controversial rap superstar Tupac Shakur was a former member of this group. Name the group.

253. Besides being a rap star and Oscar-nominated actress, she's also a record executive. Who is she?

254. This rap artist's single "Cop Killer", featured on his 1993 album, *Body Count,* was removed from his album after much controversy. He also starred in the Mario Van Peebles' movie, "New Jack City". Who is he?

255. This crossover rapper hit the scene with the hit, "Bust a Move" and wrote Tone-Loc's huge hit, "Funky Cold Medina". Who is he?

256. This late rap artist was criticized after making statements for an L.A.P.D. officer involved in the Rodney King beating.

257. Who are Sandy Denton, Cheryl James and Dee Dee Roper more commonly known as?

Rap

258. This artist's 1987 album *Saturday Night* and 1988's *Smoke Some Kill* had city officials demanding the albums be removed from record stores. Name the artist.

259. Then-Presidential candidate Bill Clinton attacked this rapper's album, accusing her of hatred and urging African-Americans to kill Caucasians. Name the artist and the album.

African-American Music Trivia

IT'S A "RAP" *Answers page 121*

Complete the following rap song titles.

260. Cop _____

261. Slow _____

262. California _____

263. Murder Was _____

264. Push _____

265. King _____

266. Strawberry _____

267. Dog Is _____

268. Hard _____

269. Don't Sweat _____

270. Passing _____

271. Freaks Come _____

Rap

272. By the Time _____

273. White Lines _____

274. The Humpty _____

275. Knockin' _____

276. Roxanne, _____

277. U.N.I. _____

278. Too Legit _____

279. Crack _____

A.K.A. (Also Known As) *Answers page 122*

Give the real name of these rap artists.

280. "Schooly D"

281. "Grandmaster Flash"

282. "Ice-T"

283. "Rodney O"

284. "Chubb Rock"

285. "Run"

286. "DMC"

287. "Intelligent Hoodlum"

288. "MC Brains"

289. "Chill Rob G"

290. "Professor Griff"

291. "Easy-E"

Rap

292. "Ice Cube"

293. "Yo-Yo"

294. "Blowfly"

295. "Kool Moe Dee"

296. "M.C. Ren"

297. "Dr. Dre"

298. "M.C. Lyte"

299. "Doug E. Fresh"

THE BLUES

NAME THE ARTIST *Answers page 122*

300. This songwriter sang the hit, "Night Time Is the Right Time".

301. This Chicago-born artist began playing classical flute before changing over to the amplified harmonica. Who is it?

302. This Blues artist perfected his guitar skills as he served his stint at a reform school for running away from home. Who is he?

303. This early Blues artist was known for having a bottle in one hand and a bottleneck in the other. Who is he?

304. Japanese fans call him "The Mellow Blues Genius". Who is he?

305. This artist got his nickname after a hoboing accident in the early 1930s.

306. Eric Clapton recorded this artist's "Personal Manager" solo for guitar note-for-note on a song by Cream entitled, "Stranger's Brew". Name the artist.

The Blues

307. John and Alan Lomax discovered this Blues artist in 1933 while he was in the Louisiana State Penitentiary. Who was he?

308. This artist plays harmonica turned upside down in a "rack". Who is he?

309. This artist's jug band style was a staple of early Blues music by the Grateful Dead. Name the artist.

310. This blues guitarist appeared with Queen of Soul Aretha Franklin in the 1980's movie, *The Blues Brothers*.

311. This Blues singer's two number one hits were "Good Rockin' Tonight" and "All She Wants To Do Is Rock".

312. This Bluesman was working as a Pullman porter when he was hired by Victor records in 1928. Who was he?

313. Two of this artist's best-known ballads are "Since I Met You Baby" and "I Almost Lost My Mind". Who is he?

314. This artist penned the Ray Charles hit, "Hit the Road, Jack".

African-American Music Trivia

315. This artist's playing partner in the 1930s was Charley Patton. Name the artist.

316. This Blues superstar, known as "The King of Blues", developed a vibrato for blues guitars. Who is he?

317. This artist is known for his whoops, hollers and fox-chasing imitations. Name the artist.

318. This Bluesman was one of the founding members of the group, The Headhunters, along with Little Walter & Muddy Waters. Who was he?

319. This blues great served as B.B. King's chauffer and valet before his career in Blues music took off. Name the artist.

320. This songwriter is considered the best-known Blues songwriter in music history. Name the artist.

321. The Blues singer debuted on the Rhythm & Blues chart in 1964 with a song entitled, "You Were Wrong". Name the artist.

322. This Blues artist spent 5 years in prison in the 1940s for killing his wife. One of his early hits was entitled, "Penitentiary Moan Blues". Name the artist.

The Blues

323. Two of this artist's LPs are *The Devil Is a Busy Man* and *Sad and Lonesome*. Name the artist.

324. Elvis Presley stated at one time that this Bluesman was one of his major influences. Who was he referring to?

A.K.A. (Also Known As) *Answers page 123*

Provide the stage name for the following blues artists.

325. Robert Hicks

326. James A. Lane

327. Milton Campbell

328. Amos Blackmore

329. Sam Hopkins

330. Albert Luandrew

331. Maybelle Smith

332. John Lee Williamson

333. John Adam Estes

334. John T. Smith

335. Francis Blackwell

336. Marion Walter Jacob

The Blues

337. William Lee Conley Broonzy

338. McKinley Morganfield

339. Thomas Andrew Dorsey

340. Iverson Minter

341. Booker T. Washington White

342. Albert Clemens

343. Charles Arthur Burnett

344. Robert McCollum

MOVIE SOUNDTRACKS AND TELEVISION THEME SONGS

African-American Music Trivia

YOU NAME IT *Answers page 124*

345. Donny Hathaway sang the theme for this '70s CBS sitcom.

346. This group performed the title song for the 1976 movie, *Car Wash*.

347. This Grammy Award Winner sang the title song for the James Bond movie, *A License To Kill*.

348. This duo sang the title song for the 1981 movie, *Endless Love*.

349. Lionel Richie sang this song for the 1985 movie, *White Knights*.

350. EU performed "Da Butt" for this Spike Lee film.

351. This dynamic duo sang the love theme "Without You" for Bill Cosby's movie, *Leonard, Part VI* as well as the song, "A Whole New World" for the 1992 Disney animated motion picture, *Aladdin*. Name the duo.

352. What 1971 movie was the late Sammy Davis, Jr.'s song, "The Candy Man" featured in?

Movie Soundtracks & Television Theme Songs

353. This actress/singer wrote the theme song for the NBC sitcom, *A Different World*, starring Lisa Bonét.

354. Curtis Mayfield's "Freddie's Dead" was one of the songs featured in this 1972 "Blaxploitation" film.

355. Janet Jackson and Luther Vandross performed a duet for the movie, *Mo' Money*, starring Damon Wayans. Name the song.

356. This song, performed by the late Whitney Houston, but originally recorded by Chaka Khan, was featured in the 1992 box office blockbuster, *The Bodyguard*. Name the song.

357. This song was performed by British artist Seal and was featured in the 1995 movie, *Batman Forever*. Name the song.

358. Hip-Hop Queen Mary J. Blige sang this song in the 1995 hit movie, *Waiting to Exhale* by novelist Terry McMillan. Name the song.

359. This duo's remake of Roberta Flack and Donnie Hathaway's "Where Is The Love", was featured in the 1995 movie, *Dead Presidents* starring Larenz Tate and Bokeem Woodbine. Name the duo.

African-American Music Trivia

360. This song was performed by songbird Toni Braxton and produced by musical genius Kenny "Babyface" Edmonds for the 1992 movie, *Boomerang* starring Eddie Murphy and Robin Givens.

361. Legendary guitarist Willie Hutch composed, arranged and produced the soundtrack to this 1973 "Blaxploitation" movie. Name the movie.

362. Diana Ross performed this song for the 1975 movie, *Mahogany* in which she starred with Billy Dee Williams. Name the song.

363. This family group sang the song for the 1975 movie, *Let's Do It Again*.

364. Barry White wrote the score for this 1974 thriller. Name the movie.

365. This jazz master provided the opening theme for the 1980s series, *Moonlighting*.

366. Marvin Gaye's hit, "I Heard It Through the Grapevine" was featured in this 1983 movie.

367. The group Silk sang this song acapella in the 1994 movie, *Blankman*.

Movie Soundtracks & Television Theme Songs

368. Bobby McFerrin's 1988 hit, "Don't Worry, Be Happy" was featured in this 1988 movie starring Tom Cruise.

369. This female vocalist/actress sang the title tracks for the 1980 movie, *Fame* and the 1983 movie, *Flashdance*. Who is she?

370. What song of the Jimi Hendrix Experience was featured in the 1994 movie, *In The Name of the Father?*

371. This song by Sir Mix-A-Lot and Mudhoney was featured in this 1993 movie.

372. Paul Robeson's take of "Ol' Man River" was featured in this Rodgers & Hammerstein 1951 musical.

373. Morris Day and The Time performed a song about a certain kind of "love" in Prince's 1984 motion picture, *Purple Rain*. Name the song.

374. The late singer/actress Nell Carter sang the opening theme for this 1980s sitcom she starred in. Name the sitcom.

375. Tamia, Brandy, Gladys Knight and Chaka Khan sang this song "Missing You" for this 1996 movie about four female bank robbers starring Queen Latifah, Jada Pinkett-Smith, Vivica A. Fox and Kimberly Elise.

African-American Music Trivia

376. This actress/singer sang the theme song for the 1970s hit sitcom, *The Jeffersons*. Who is she?

377. The song, "U Will Know" was featured in the 1994 movie, *Jason's Lyric,* starring Allen Payne and Jada Pinkett-Smith. Name the group that performed it.

378. Former Miss America/singer/actress Vanessa Williams sang the song, "Colors of the Wind", which was featured in this 1995 Disney animated motion picture. Name the motion picture.

379. Sade performed this song for this 1994 movie starring Demi Moore, Woody Harrelson and Robert Redford.

380. The song, "Will You Be There" by Michael Jackson, was featured in this 1993 movie about a whale. Name the movie.

381. Superstar Janet Jackson co-wrote and performed this Academy Award-nominated song featured in the 1993 movie, *Poetic Justice,* starring Jackson and the late rap superstar Tupac Shakur. Name the song.

382. One of superstar Patti LaBelle's songs was featured in the 1984 Eddie Murphy movie, *Beverly Hills Cop.* Name the song.

Movie Soundtracks & Television Theme Songs

383. O.C. Smith recorded the song, "Blowin' Your Mind" for this 1972 movie. Name the movie.

384. Velvet-voiced crooner Nat King Cole sang this song for the 1958 movie of the same name, which was based on composer W.C. Handy's life. Name the movie.

385. The song, "Rock the Boat" was featured in the 1994 movie, *Carlito's Way* starring superstar Al Pacino. Name the group who sang the song.

386. The beautiful and multi-talented actress/singer Lena Horne sang the title song to her 1943 movie of the same name.

387. This composer's music was used for the 1959 movie, *Anatomy of a Murder*. Name the composer.

388. Forever-young Tina Turner sang the theme for this 1995 James Bond movie. Name the movie.

389. This song by Inner Circle is the theme song for the television show *Cops* and was featured in the 1995 movie of the same name, starring Will Smith and Martin Lawrence. Name the song.

MULTIPLE MUSIC GENRES

African-American Music Trivia

DEARLY DEPARTED *Answers page 126*

390. Singer/songwriter Donny Hathaway died when he jumped from of this hotel's 15th floor window in 1979. Name the hotel.

391. Jackie Wilson suffered a stroke while performing on stage in this city on September 25, 1975. He remained hospitalized for almost 9 years following it. Eventually, it ended his life. Name the city where he has performing and the date of his death.

392. Soul crooner Sam Cooke died on December 11, 1964. How did he depart this life?

393. Rock guitarist Jimi Hendrix died from a heroin overdose and suffocation in London, England on this date.

394. Blues guitarist/pianist Andrew "Smokey" Hogg died on this date from a hemorrhaging ulcer. Name the date.

395. Blues songwriter Willie Dixon died in Burbank, California on June 29, 1952. What happened to him?

396. Singer Minnie Riperton, known for her six-octave vocal range, died on this date due to breast cancer. Name the date.

Multiple Music Genres

397. Controversial rap superstar, Tupac Amaru Shakur, was shot on September 7, 1996 after attending the Mike Tyson/Bruce Seldon boxing match in Las Vegas, Nevada and died six days later. Name the record executive who was the driver of the vehicle that both he and Shakur were shot in and the record company he was chairman of.

398. Rhythm & Blues entertainer Chuck Willis, best known for his recording, *"C.C. Rider"* died April 10, 1958 due to complications from this. What was it?

399. Soul saxophonist King Curtis was stabbed to death outside his apartment home August 14, 1971. What east coast state did he live in?

400. Dancer & "Rat Pack" member, Sammy Davis, Jr. succumbed to this disease on May 15, 1990. What was it?

401. Singer Otis Redding, famous for his smash hit, "Sittin' On the Dock of the Bay", died in a plane crash December 10, 1967 when the plane he was a passenger in, plunged into a lake a few miles away from Madison, Wisconsin. Name the lake.

402. Famed jazz pianist, Thelonious "Sphere" Monk died after he suffered a stroke February 17, 1982. What city was he in when he died?

African-American Music Trivia

403. Guitar Slim was in this city when he died of pneumonia February 7, 1959. Where was he?

404. Philippe Wynne, lead singer of R&B group The Spinners, died July 13, 1984 after suffering a heart attack while performing at this nightclub in Oakland, California. Name the club.

405. Velvet-voiced crooner Nat King Cole entered a Santa Monica hospital January 25, 1965 to have this organ removed. Less than one month later, he died. Name the organ removed and the date of his death.

406. Singer Larry "Billy" Stewart, known for the 1962 hit, "Reap What You Sow", died January 17, 1970 when the car he was in, along with band members Norman Rich, William Cathey and Rico Hightower, left Interstate 95 and plunged into the Neuse River in North Carolina. What are the names of the band members who perished with him?

407. Percy Mayfield died August 11, 1984 of a heart attack. He was one day shy of something. What was it?

408. Big Joe Turner, R&B artist famous for the 1954 hit, "Shake, Rattle & Roll" and many other hits, died of this November 24, 1985. What was it?

Multiple Music Genres

409. Singer Shorty Long, famous for "Devil with a Blue Dress", died June 29, 1969. How and where did he depart this life?

410. Linda Jones died March 14, 1972 after collapsing backstage at the famed Apollo Theater. What did she die of?

411. Bluesman Z.Z. Hill, famous for his hit, "Down Home Blues", died April 27, 1984 as a result of this. What was it?

412. Former Supreme Florence Ballard died on this date in Detroit, Michigan after suffering a heart attack. Name the date.

413. Famed Motown singer Tammi Terrell, known for her famous duets with fellow Motown genius Marvin Gaye ("Ain't Nothing Like the Real Thing"), died March 16, 1970 because of this disease diagnosed in 1967 after collapsing on stage. What ended Tammi's life?

414. Blues legend Bessie Smith died September 26, 1937 after sustaining injuries in a car accident in Clarksdale, Mississippi. She was on tour in a show at the time. Name the show.

African-American Music Trivia

415. Blues great Gertrude "Ma" Rainey, known for the hits "Don't Fish in My Sea" and "Farewell Daddy Blues", died December 22, 1939 in Columbus, Georgia of this. What was it?

416. Jazz singer Little Willie John, known for the 1955 hit, "Grits Ain't Groceries", was convicted in May 1966 of manslaughter for stabbing a man to death. He was serving time at the Washington State Penitentiary and died on May 26, 1968 of this. What was it?

417. The Reverend Thomas A. Dorsey, writer of the gospel masterpiece "Precious Lord, Take My Hand" died on January 23, 1993 at the age of 93 in Chicago of this mind-crippling disease. What was it?

418. The Reverend Gary Davis, who was known as one of the most influential 12-string guitar players, died after suffering a heart attack on May 5, 1972 while on his way to this. Where was he going?

419. Renowned jazz vocalist Sarah Vaughn, known for many hits, including the 1959 hit "Broken-Hearted Melody", died April 3, 1990 of this illness. What was it?

Multiple Music Genres

420. Leadbelly, well-known folk music legend known for "The Boll Weevil" and "Goodnight, Irene", died December 6, 1949 while he was a patient at Bellevue Hospital in New York City. What claimed his life?

ANSWERS

RHYTHM AND BLUES/SOUL PART I
The Early Years 1950-1965

NAME THE ARTIST *page 18*
1. a
2. c
3. b
4. a
5. a
6. d
7. b
8. b
9. b
10. a

WHAT WERE OUR ORIGINAL NAMES? *Page 21*
11. The Mellotones
12. The Harlem Queens
13. The Sentimental Four
14. Little Miss and The Muffets
15. The Poets
16. The Four Pennies
17. The Matadors
18. The Four Gents
19. The Artettes
20. The Four Clovers

Answers

NAME THE YEAR *page 22*
21. b
22. b
23. a
24. b
25. b
26. c
27. c
28. c
29. a
30. d
31. c
32. c
33. d
34. a
35. a
36. b
37. d
38. d
39. b
40. c

THE NAME GAME AND BIRTHPLACE *page 27*

41. c
    41a. a
42. b
    42a. b
43. b
    43a. b
44. c
    44a. b
45. c
    45a. a
46. c
    46c. a
47. b
    47a. d
48. c
    48a. c
49. a
    49a. a
50. c
    50a. c
51. c
    51a. c
52. b
    52a. b
53. c
    53a. b
54. c
    54a. d

Answers

THE NAME GAME AND BIRTHPLACE cont'd *page 27*

55. b
   55a. d
56. a
   56a. c
57. b
   57a. b
58. a
   58a. b
59. c
   59a. b
60. a
   60a. d

RHYTHM AND BLUES/SOUL PART II
The Next 15 years 1966-1981

NUMBER ONES *page 38*

61. d
62. c
63. b
64. c
65. c
66. a
67. c
68. d
69. b
70. b
71. d
72. c
73. c
74. c
75. d
76. a
77. d
78. d
79. d
80. d
81. a
82. c
83. d
84. b
85. c

Answers

GRAB BAG *page 44*
- 86. Quincy Jones
- 87. Chapter 8
- 88. 1976
- 89. Soul Train
- 90. Mother, Father, Sister, Brother
- 91. Tavares
- 92. The Sylvers
- 93. The S.O.S. Band
- 94. Sly and the Family Stone
- 95. Curtom Records
- 96. Hotter Than July
- 97. Shalamar
- 98. Where is the Love?
- 99. Mercy, Mercy, Me
- 100. Russell Thompkins, Jr.

African-American Music Trivia

RHYTHM AND BLUES/SOUL PART III
End of the Century 1982 to 1996

IN THE KNOW *page 48*

101. Jimmy Jam and Terry Lewis
102. Toni Braxton
103. Back In Stride
104. Theodore "Teddy" Pendergrass
105. Guy
106. Lenny Kravitz
107. Roxie Roker
108. Hazel
109. Sade
110. 1984
111. Gerald and Eddie Levert
112. Stone Love
113. Grand Rapids, Michigan
114. Club Nouveau
115. Raspberry
116. Ralph (Tresvant), Bobby (Brown), Michael (Bivens), Ricky (Bell), Ronald (DeVoe)
117. R. Kelly
118. Vanity (Denise), Brenda and Susan
119. Winner in You
120. The Mary Jane Girls
121. Clifton Davis
122. Iman
123. En Vogue

Answers

124. Grace Jones
125. Jacci McGhee
126. Brandy Norwood
127. Shanice
128. Wilson
129. After 7
130. Slide

MATCH-UP *page 52*
Young Hearts Run Free (Candi Staton-Nixon)
Car Wash (Rose Royce)
Smiling Faces (Undisputed Truth)
Boogie Nights (Heatwave)
Funky Worm (The Ohio Players)
Somewhere In My Lifetime (Phyllis Hyman)
Strawberry Letter 23 (Brothers Johnson)
Reunited (Peaches and Herb)
Give Me Just A Little More Time (Chairmen of the Board)
The Love I Lost (Harold Melvin and the Blue Notes)
River Deep, Mountain High (Tina Turner)
Give It to Me, Baby (Rick James)
Somebody's Been Sleeping in My Bed (Johnny Taylor)
Love Ballad (L.T.D.)
The Lonely One (Special Delivery)

AMERICAN JAZZ ERA

JAZZ GRAB BAG *page 56*
- 131. Dizzy Gillespie
- 132. "My Appreciation" or "Where You Lay Your Head"
- 133. Lonnie Johnson
- 134. Maceo Parker
- 135. Patti Austin
- 136. Archie Shepp
- 137. 1944
- 138. Casino de Paris
- 139. Jimmy McGriff
- 140. Eric Allan Dolphy
- 141. Classical piano
- 142. Charles Melvin "Cootie" Williams
- 143. Tenor and alto saxophone and flute
- 144. 1956
- 145. Kenny Kirkland
- 146. Theodore Walker "Sonny" Rollins
- 147. Eclipse
- 148. Stanley Jordan
- 149. 1935
- 150. Sidney Bechet
- 151. Fritz Jones
- 152. Terence Blanchard
- 153. Ray Brown
- 154. Freddie Hubbard

Answers

JAZZ GRAB BAG cont'd *page 56*

155. Bessie Smith
156. 1933
157. Violin and cello
158. Miles Davis
159. 1981
160. Patrice Rushen
161. Ray Brown and Charlie Smith
162. The trumpet
163. Elvin Jones
164. Errol Garner
165. 16
166. Milt Hinton
167. Lester Brown
168. Jaki Byard
169. 1958
170. Oscar Pettiford
171. Nogales, Arizona
172. 76
173. Buddy Bolden
174. Love and Kisses
175. The Seventeen Messengers
176. Ron Carter
177. 1943
178. 1937
179. Louis Armstrong Big Band
180. The Modern Jazz Quartet

AFRICAN-AMERICAN GOSPEL

WHO ARE WE? *Page 64*

181. Tremaine Hawkins
182. Vanessa Bell-Armstrong
183. The Five Blind Boys of Mississippi
184. Barnes & Brown
185. Tiffanie and Tammy Morgan, Jennifer and Angela Tooley
186. Brother Joe May
187. The Barrett Sisters
188. Golden Eagle Gospel Singers
189. Philip Bailey
190. Mahalia Jackson
191. Albertina Walker
192. The Dixie Hummingbirds
193. Inez Andrews
194. The Banks Brothers
195. Benjamin and Priscilla
196. Helen Baylor
197. The Pilgrim Travelers
198. Margaret Bell
199. The Charioteers
200. Sandra Crouch
201. Professor Alex Bradford
202. Willie Banks
203. The Rance Allen Group
204. The Clark Sisters

Answers

THE DISCO ERA

DISCO SONG TITLES *page 70*
- 205. Dance
- 206. Missing and Angel
- 207. Survive
- 208. Inferno
- 209. Hangover
- 210. Times
- 211. Greatest Dancer
- 212. You Get Enough
- 213. Nights
- 214. Sesame
- 215. Lady
- 216. Dance
- 217. Mortis
- 218. Play
- 219. Freak
- 220. You Baby
- 221. Bell
- 222. Tonight
- 223. C.A.
- 224. Mighty Real
- 225. Real
- 226. Oogie
- 227. Marmalade
- 228. Thing
- 229. Off

African-American Music Trivia

DISCO SONG TITLES cont'd page 68
- 230. Stuff
- 231. This Way
- 232. Night
- 233. Love
- 234. You

RAP

"RAP" IT UP *page 74*
- 235. Rapper's Delight by The Sugarhill Gang
- 236. I Got a Man
- 237. No More Mr. Nice Guy
- 238. Doug E. Fresh and the Get Fresh Crew
- 239. Arrested Development
- 240. Ladies Love Cool James
- 241. Big Daddy Kane
- 242. Kriss-Kross
- 243. X-Clan
- 244. Stanley Kirk Burrell
- 245. The Lynch Mob
- 246. Biz Markie
- 247. Baby Got Back
- 248. Kurtis Blow
- 249. Melle Mel, Rahiem, Mr. Ness, Cowboy and Kid Creole
- 250. Candyman
- 251. World Class Wreckin' Cru
- 252. Digital Underground
- 253. Queen Latifah

Answers

"RAP" IT UP cont'd *page 74*
- 254. Ice-T
- 255. Young M.C.
- 256. Easy-E
- 257. Salt-N-Peppa and Spinderella
- 258. Schooly D
- 259. Sister Souljah, 360 Degrees of Power

IT'S A "RAP" *page 78*
- 260. Killer
- 261. And Sexy
- 262. Love
- 263. The Case
- 264. It
- 265. Of Rock
- 266. Lane
- 267. A Dog
- 268. Times
- 269. The Technique
- 270. Me By
- 271. Out at Night
- 272. I Get to Arizona
- 273. Don't Don't Do It
- 274. Dance
- 275. Boots
- 276. Roxanne
- 277. T.Y.
- 278. To Quit
- 279. Attack

African-American Music Trivia

A.K.A. (Also Known As) *page 80*
- 280. Jesse B. Weaver, Jr.
- 281. Joseph Saddler
- 282. Tracy Morrow
- 283. Rodney Oliver
- 284. Richard Simpson
- 285. Joseph Simmons
- 286. Darryl McDaniels
- 287. Percy Chapman
- 288. James DeShannon Davis
- 289. Rob Frazier
- 290. Richard Griffin
- 291. Eric Wright
- 292. O'Shea Jackson
- 293. Yolanda Whitaker
- 294. Clarence Reid
- 295. Mohandas DeWese
- 296. Lorenzo Patterson
- 297. André Young
- 298. Lana Moorer
- 299. Doug E. Davis

THE BLUES

NAME THE ARTIST *page 84*
- 300. Roosevelt Sykes
- 301. Paul Butterfield
- 302. Luther Johnson

Answers

NAME THE ARTIST cont'd *page 84*
- 303. Furry Lewis
- 304. Fenton Robinson
- 305. Peg Leg Sam
- 306. Albert King
- 307. Leadbelly
- 308. Dr. Isiah Ross
- 309. Cannon's Jug Stompers
- 310. Matt "Guitar" Murphy
- 311. Wynonie Harris
- 312. Robert Wilkins
- 313. Ivory Joe Hunter
- 314. Percy Mayfield
- 315. Eddie James "Son" House, Jr.
- 316. B.B. King
- 317. Sonny Terry
- 318. Jimmy Hunter
- 319. Bobby "Blue" Bland
- 320. Willie Dixon
- 321. Z.Z. Hill
- 322. Alger "Texas" Alexander
- 323. Sunnyland Slim
- 324. Arthur "Big Boy" Crudup

A.K.A. (Also Known As) *page 88*
- 325. Barbecue Bob
- 326. Jimmy Rogers
- 327. Little Milton

African-American Music Trivia

A.K.A. (Also Known As) cont'd *page 88*
- 328. Junior Wells
- 329. Lightnin' Hopkins
- 330. Sunnyland Slim
- 331. Big Maybelle
- 332. Sonny Boy
- 333. Sleepy John Estes
- 334. Funny Papa Smith
- 335. Scrapper Blackwell
- 336. Little Walter
- 337. Big Bill Broonzy
- 338. Muddy Waters
- 339. Georgia Tom Dorsey
- 340. Louisiana Red
- 341. Bukka White
- 342. Cripple Clarence Lofton
- 343. Howlin' Wolf
- 344. Robert Nighthawk

MOVIE SOUNDTRACKS/TELEVISION THEME SONGS

YOU NAME IT *page 92*
- 345. Maude
- 346. Rose Royce
- 347. Gladys Knight
- 348. Lionel Richie and Diana Ross
- 349. Say You, Say Me
- 350. School Daze

Answers

YOU NAME IT cont'd *page 92*

351. Peabo Bryson and Regina Belle
352. Willy Wonka and The Chocolate Factory
353. Dawnn Lewis
354. Superfly
355. The Best Things in Life are Free
356. I'm Every Woman
357. Kiss from a Rose
358. Not Gon' Cry
359. Jesse & Trina B
360. Give You My Heart
361. Willie Hutch
362. Do You Know Where You're Going To?
363. The Staple Singers
364. Together Brothers
365. Al Jarreau
366. The Big Chill
367. Cry On
368. Cocktail
369. Irene Cara
370. Voodoo Chile
371. Judgment Night
372. Show Boat
373. Jungle Love
374. Gimmie A Break
375. Set It Off
376. Ja'Net DuBois
377. Black Men United

378. Pocahontas
379. Indecent Exposure
380. Free Willy
381. Again
382. New Attitude
383. Shaft's Big Score
384. St. Louis Blues
385. The Hues Corporation
386. Stormy Weather
387. Duke Ellington
388. Goldeneye
389. Bad Boys

MULTIPLE MUSIC GENRES

DEARLY DEPARTED *page 100*
390. New York City Essex House Hotel
391. Camden, New Jersey: January 21, 1984
392. Shot to death
393. September 18, 1970
394. May 1, 1960
395. Heart attack
396. July 19, 1979
397. Marion "Suge" Knight; Death Row Records
398. Car accident
399. New York
400. Throat cancer
401. Lake Monona

Answers

DEARLY DEPARTED cont'd *page 98*
402. Englewood, New Jersey
403. New York
404. Ivey's Nightclub
405. Left lung, February 15, 1965
406. Norman Rich, William Cathey and Rico Hightower
407. His 64th birthday
408. Kidney failure
409. Boating accident in the Great Lakes
410. Diabetes
411. Blood clot to the heart
412. February 22, 1976
413. Brain tumor
414. Broadway Rastus
415. Heart attack
416. Pneumonia
417. Alzheimer's Disease
418. To a concert
419. Lung cancer
420. Lou Gehrig's Disease

African-American Music Trivia

SOURCE REFERENCES
(For Accuracy Purposes Only - In Alphabetical Order)

"All Music Guide, Second Edition"
by Chris Woodstra & Vladimir Bogdanov
Edited by Michael Erlewine

Columbia House Records and Tapes

Personal Record Collection of Alicia Woodfork-Wilkerson

Rolling Stone Magazine

"Stars of Soul and Rhythm & Blues"
by Lee Hildebrand

"This Day In African-American Music"
by Ted Holland

www.ingramcontent.com/pod-product-compliance
Lightning Source LLC
Chambersburg PA
CBHW050559300426
44112CB00013B/1985